Original title:
The Meaning of Life: A Work in Progress

Copyright © 2025 Creative Arts Management OÜ
All rights reserved.

Author: Nathaniel Blackwood
ISBN HARDBACK: 978-1-80566-254-9
ISBN PAPERBACK: 978-1-80566-549-6

Flickers of Hope

In a world of half-baked plans,
I trip over my own two hands.
Chasing dreams on wobbly feet,
Finding joy in clumsy defeat.

A squirrel stole my sandwich, bold,
As I ponder mysteries untold.
Life's a circus, laughter loud,
And I'm the jester in the crowd.

Bridges to Nowhere

I built a bridge to the moon's bright face,
But forgot to leave an empty space.
With each step, I paint the air,
In a dance of mischief and flair.

Traffic cones in a cosmic line,
Guide lost souls when they dine.
Mapping routes of silly pranks,
We find joy in life's blank banks.

Seeds of Reflection

Planting seeds in my quirky head,
They sprout ideas that laugh and spread.
With every thought, a flower blooms,
In a garden of giggles, life resumes.

Yet some weeds pop up, quite rude,
Cackling 'bout my midday food.
I grab my shovel, give a wink,
And giggle at the plants that think.

Beyond the Horizon's Gaze

Past the hills where laughter's spun,
I wander under a silly sun.
Every step, a twist and shout,
With sunshine giggles all about.

I meet a goat with a rainbow tie,
Who waves to clouds, and asks them why.
We sip on lemonade so sweet,
As life dances to its own heartbeat.

Spiral of Time

Every tick, a question's born,
Am I the hare or the worn?
Chasing shadows, laughing loud,
Are we just a saucy crowd?

Round and round, the clock combines,
Eating snacks, sipping wines.
With every turn, a new delight,
We trip and fall, then take flight.

Chronicle of the Unsung

In the corners, they all dwell,
Forgotten tales, a silent bell.
Dancing mice, in tiny shoes,
Sharing secrets, none we choose.

Waffle makers hum a tune,
While socks go missing—who'd have known?
Each unsung hero's full of quirks,
Finding joy in humble works.

Boundless Horizons

Off we go, to lands unseen,
Chasing dreams, not quite obscene.
Surfing clouds or riding bikes,
All we need is pizza slices.

Up we float on kites of laughter,
Searching for the wind—what's after?
Through boundless skies, we spin and twirl,
Life's a game, let's give it a whirl!

Threads of Connection

Tangled webs of fate we weave,
Grandmas knitting dreams, believe!
With every stitch, a tale we spin,
Of messy hair and goofy grins.

So raise a toast, let laughter soar,
One big hug, forever more.
In the fabric of this show,
We find love in the ebb and flow.

Resonance of the Soul

In the rhythm of our days, we play,
Finding purpose in our own quirky way.
Each blunder, a step in a dance so odd,
Life's a sitcom, not a well-trodden road.

We chase dreams like cats chasing their tails,
In a world full of tales and clumsy fails.
With laughter as our guide, we trip and glide,
Sipping coffee while surfing the wild tide.

Veils of Illusion

Behind each curtain, there's a silly show,
With clowns and balloons and a sprinkle of dough.
To decipher the script is a riotous game,
Where truth wears a mask, but it's still the same.

We strut like peacocks, a feathery sight,
Wishing for thrills in the midst of the night.
But underneath sparkles, we all share a plight,
In this circus of life, we laugh at the fright.

Prisms of Possibility

Life's a prism of colors, wildly untamed,
With shades of confusion, we're all unashamed.
We mix silly pigments, let chaos ignite,
Creating our canvases from day into night.

Every choice is a splash, a stroke without regret,
In a gallery where quiet artists fret.
Let's paint a masterpiece with strokes of the jest,
For in laughter, dear friends, we find our zest.

Tides of Transformation

Waves of change crash upon our shores,
Carrying tales of quirky galores.
We surf through the whirlpools of fumbles and grins,
In the tide's wild embrace, our laughter begins.

With sand between toes and plans that unroll,
Each misstep a giggle, each stumble a role.
We ebb and we flow, in this vast, silly sea,
For the journey is laughter, and laughs set us free.

Sculpting the Unknown

With clay in hand, I shape the day,
A lumpy mess, come what may.
My masterpiece, it seems, is shy,
It giggles loud as it says goodbye.

I tried to mold a smile so wide,
Instead, I got a penguin's glide.
Life's quirks turn figures into goo,
But hey, who knew? I like 'em blue!

Each twist and turn, a dance of fate,
My sculpture's done—oh wait, I'm late!
The unknown calls, with splashes bright,
Let's grasp the brush, and paint it right!

A Tapestry of Purpose

Threads of laughter stitch the seams,
A tapestry woven from wild dreams.
Each patch a story, some bright, some gray,
Pull a loose string, watch it sway!

I thought I'd craft a grand design,
Yet each knot's a punchline divine.
Embracing chaos, colors collide,
At least it's warm when I hide inside!

Patterns emerge, then fray and break,
A quilt to cover each silly mistake.
With every twist and absurd embrace,
Life's woven mess becomes our grace.

Navigating the Currents of Fate

A boat of rubber on a wild stream,
Paddles are flippers, it's all a dream.
I steer with gusto, or so I claim,
But all that's clear are the ducks at game.

Waves crash lightly, splashing my face,
Oops! I googled the wrong kind of grace.
Life's a river, twists and spins,
And I'm just here for the boat race wins!

Casting nets with a hopeful heart,
I catch a shoe instead of art.
But laughter leads, I'll take the bait,
Rowing along, just tempting fate!

The Puzzle of Every Breath

A jigsaw piece labeled 'Who am I?'
With edges straight and colors awry.
I search for corners, now here, now there,
Keys to the mystery, everywhere!

Each breath I take, a square on the board,
Some fit like magic, others I hoard.
Life's a conundrum, a laugh-out-loud chore,
Like finding a sock in a never-closed door!

The picture forms, a portrait absurd,
A cat in a hat, haven't you heard?
Piece by piece, we fit in the space,
Every giggle reveals our place.

Dance of Uncertainty

In a twirl with doubts, I spin so wide,
Did I eat the last cookie? Oh, what a ride!
With every wrong step, I laugh and trip,
Life's a party, grab your snack and dip!

The cha-cha of choices, oh what a scene,
Do I wear polka dots, or stick with green?
Each move is a gamble, a whimsical chance,
So let's tango with fate, let's all take a dance!

Canvas of Experience

Splash of colors, oh what a mess,
Is that mustard or paint? I can't guess!
Each brushstroke I make, a smile and a frown,
Art from my chaos, I wear like a crown.

My canvas is busy, with doodles and laughs,
I sketch out my dinner and my weird paths.
With a wink to the future, I'll color outside,
Life's a masterpiece, come, take a ride!

Navigating Through Chaos

With my map upside down, I sail the sea,
Is that a wave I see, or just my tea?
Captain of silly, I steer with a grin,
Full speed ahead, let the madness begin!

In a boat made of soup, I float with style,
Dodging the turbulence, oh, what a while!
Each splash is a chuckle, each wave is a dance,
Through storms of confusion, I'll always take a chance!

Embracing the Unknown

Wearing my mismatched socks, I tap my feet,
What's hiding around the corner? A pizza treat?
The unknown is a friend, with surprises galore,
Let's open the door, who could ask for more?

I juggle my worries, they giggle and bounce,
Each silly distraction, I laugh and announce.
With friends by my side, we chase after thrills,
In the realm of the strange, my heart surely fills!

Chasing Shadows of Tomorrow

In search of dreams that dance and play,
We trip on thoughts that lead astray.
With socks that clash in vibrant hues,
We chase the whims, the laughs, the clues.

Each day a puzzle, pieces lost,
We juggle life despite the cost.
With coffee spills and mismatched shoes,
We strike a pose, then laugh and lose.

Plans made in haste, like pudding pie,
We make a plan, then watch it fly.
Life's a circus, clowns in tow,
We laugh so hard, we steal the show.

Yet in the chaos, joy appears,
Like socks that disappear through years.
So let's embrace the silly tide,
And giggle loud with arms spread wide.

The Art of Becoming Whole

In mirrors cracked and views askew,
We paint ourselves a shade or two.
A splash of red, a stroke of blue,
In this mad art, we find what's true.

We wear our labels, swap them 'round,
Social tags tangled like lost-found.
A masterclass in dressing fails,
With mismatched ties and food-stained trails.

As life unfolds, we take a dive,
We laugh at how we just survive.
Becoming whole's a jolly quest,
With slip-ups turned into finesse.

So here's to all our quirky ways,
Life's a canvas, bright the days.
With every flop, a cheerful wink,
We paint our world in vibrant ink.

Echoes in the Silence

In quiet moments, thoughts collide,
Like socks in dryers, where hopes hide.
We ponder deep, then giggle loud,
Finding wisdom in the crowd.

In echoes of our morning noise,
We seek the peace, yet find the joys.
With cereal spills and dogs at play,
We find the truth in a goofy way.

The whispers of tomorrow tease,
Like leaves that dance upon the breeze.
Stories told in bursts of light,
We chase reflections day and night.

So let's embrace the sound of glee,
In silence, laughter wants to be.
From echoes vast, we start to glean,
The happy tunes that play unseen.

Mosaic of Moments

We gather crumbs of laughter bright,
A patchwork quilt beneath moonlight.
With silly faces, dances weird,
We piece together all we've cheered.

A splash of chaos, cut and paste,
In every fail, there's truth to taste.
From awkward chats to leaps of faith,
We weave our tales, both light and wraith.

Life's a puzzle with edges frayed,
Where plans dissolve like dreams delayed.
We craft our stories, stitch by stitch,
In every mishap, we find our niche.

So raise a glass, let laughter ring,
In this mosaic, our hearts take wing.
With every moment, we design,
A tapestry of joy divine.

Seasons of the Heart

In spring we plant our silly dreams,
Hoping for harvest, or so it seems.
Summer laughter, ice cream trails,
Chasing joy, where sunlight prevails.

Autumn leaves, a dance of fate,
Sweaters cozy, but can't wait!
Winter's chill brings cocoa cheers,
As we ponder our hopes and fears.

Each season spins its joyful tale,
With hiccups, stumbles, we laugh, we wail.
Life's a ride, both bright and stark,
With moments that light up the dark.

So grab your gloves, don't take it too serious,
Embrace the chaos, it's all quite curious.
In our hearts, the seasons play,
A wobbly dance, come what may!

Tapestry of Time

Threads of laughter, tangled fate,
Stitching stories, we navigate.
Weave in chaos, and a thread of peace,
Unraveling moments, never cease.

A patch of joy, a swath of woe,
Colors blend, and spirits glow.
A misstep here, a playful snare,
In this fabric, we find our flair.

Knots of wisdom, frayed with fun,
Stitches that catch the careless run.
Each pattern strange, yet so divine,
Life's odd quilt, a grand design.

So hold the needle, sow with glee,
Embrace the wild, let humor be.
In this tapestry, we find our rhyme,
A work of art, and a sense of time!

Echoes of Yesterday

Whispers linger in the air,
Old jokes told with a goofy flair.
Hiccups from the past come back,
Carefree spirits on a joyous track.

We stumble through our memories bright,
Looking for laughter, finding delight.
In hindsight's fog, we surf and sway,
Who knew we'd turn out this way?

Oh, the blunders and quirky lines,
Each misstep adds to life's designs.
Echoes chuckle, remind us bold,
Life's a tale that's never old.

So raise a glass to those silly days,
When every cringed moment gets its praise.
In yesterday's arms, we dance and play,
With echoes that brighten our wild way!

Footprints in the Sand

Last summer's stroll left sandy trails,
With every step, our laughter sails.
Tides erase what we tried to show,
But what's a life without a little flow?

Barefoot wanderers, hearts aglow,
Chasing waves, where sea breezes blow.
The footprints fade, yet memories stay,
In the ebb and flow of our own ballet.

Sometimes we slip, and it feels like fate,
Falling sideways, but oh, isn't that great?
Life's a beach, with sunburns to teach,
Lessons in laughter, just out of reach.

So dance on the shore, let your worries blend,
With the waves and the sand, let the fun never end.
In each little footprint, we find our cheer,
This whimsical journey, let's hold it dear!

Unwritten Stories of Tomorrow

Today I tripped on a shoe,
Wondering what I should do,
Should I laugh or should I cry?
Maybe just wave my worries goodbye.

Future's pages yet to turn,
In every failure, there's a learn,
With each step, a fresh new plot,
Who knows what gold we'll have sought?

Giraffes making breakfast in bed,
Is it all in our dreams instead?
Pancakes stacked to reach the sky,
We may just need to aim high!

So let's scribble with a pen,
And dance like we're kids again,
Life's a script with twists and bends,
So grab your friends, it never ends!

Chasing Fleeting Moments

A squirrel stole my sandwich today,
Did it think it was on a buffet?
I chased it down, what a delight,
Yet it vanished, out of my sight.

Sneezed at the wrong time in class,
Thought I'd turn bright red, like grass,
But laughter erupted, oh what a scene,
The teacher rolled her eyes, so keen.

Life's a meme that's hard to catch,
Every moment feeling like a mismatch,
Juggled eggs or dropped my phone,
Why is laughter my only tone?

So here I spin like a ballerina,
Chasing joy, oh what a subpoena,
Each blink a snapshot, frame it tight,
Hold on, the fun isn't out of sight!

Whispers of the Infinite

A cat sat down to ponder all,
In the garden, it had a ball,
What's life but a long, strange game?
A never-ending quest for fame?

I asked a tree about its age,
Its rustling leaves set the stage,
"Count the rings; I've seen it all,
But squirrels still think they're ten feet tall!"

Stars twinkled like a birthday cake,
Why chase dreams, for goodness' sake?
With cosmic giggles, the moons all joke,
What's the fuss about being woke?

So let's hop on this zany ride,
With giggles and quirks on our side,
We might just find that in the fray,
The whispers guide us on our way!

Mosaic of Lessons Learned

I painted my life with neon hues,
But forgot to read the care reviews,
"Handle with laughter, keep it bright,"
And dance through each ridiculous plight.

A toaster with a mind of its own,
Hopped around, making our bread moan,
It jumped and shocked a flying fork,
Now they have formed an in-laws' cork.

Each stumble's like a puzzle piece,
A laugh, a trip, a rare release,
With every fumble, wisdom flows,
Though I still can't figure out my toes.

So let's mosaic our joys and tears,
Crafting memories out of gears,
In this circus of clowns and dreams,
Life's about laughing at silly schemes!

The Quest Beyond Certainty

In search of snacks, we wander wide,
Fumbling through choices we can't decide.
Life's like a puzzle, quite the charade,
Why choose the salad when fries are displayed?

We scribble on napkins, our grand life plan,
With doodles of cats, and a stick figure man.
Plans vanish like socks in the dryer,
But hey, we've got laughter that takes us higher!

Through detours of chaos, we trip and we spin,
Gathering moments, where to begin?
With socks mismatched and hair askew,
We stumble ahead, like a wobbly zoo.

So cheers to the journey, whatever the fate,
In the quest for wisdom, let's celebrate!
With smiles a-plenty, and giggles unbound,
In this messy adventure, pure joy can be found.

In Search of Unspoken Truths

Life's like a riddle wrapped in a clue,
As we ponder the socks that no longer are two.
In search of big questions, we snack on some fries,
While eyeing the world with skeptical eyes.

We chase down the meaning, it's slippery and sly,
Like trying to catch a butterfly flying high.
The answers we know can't fit in a jar,
Yet here we are roaming, just searching for stars.

The truths left unspoken are pranks in disguise,
Like pie in the face that gets thrown just for laughs.
We stumble on wisdom with giggles and cheer,
In this wacky pursuit of what we hold dear.

So let's raise a toast to the questions we make,
With pizza for breakfast and icing on cake!
For unspoken truths are the fun parts of dreams,
In this search for more, we find laughter's sweet beams.

Journeying Through Shadows

In shadows we travel, with snacks on the way,
Tripping on thoughts that hold sway.
Full of wild tales spun from bizarre dreams,
Where ice cream and giggles make up the themes.

Through alleys of doubt, we dance with the quirks,
Overcoming the darkness, with laughter that lurks.
With glittery wishes on the back of a cat,
Who knew that existence could be this flat?

So we tumble through hiccups and moments so bright,
Giggling at life as we take off in flight.
With dogs chasing tails and friends by our side,
Life's best interpreted as a whimsical ride.

From shadows to sunshine, we skip and we shout,
For in every adventure, there's always a route.
So here's to the journey, with laughter our guide,
With joy as our compass, we'll always abide.

Threads of Existence

Life's like a quilt, with patches so bold,
Stitched with our stories, both new and old.
With threads of confusion and patterns of fun,
We weave our existence, and hope we won't run.

In knots we encounter, new stitches appear,
Like that time we tried to make sense of our fear.
With colors so vivid and laughter so loud,
We'll layer our hearts in a chaotic shroud.

With mismatched edges and some frayed seams,
We find all the patterns that dance in our dreams.
Life's fabric is wild, with threads left undone,
But each little yarn has its place, number one!

So here's to the weaving, the tangle, the flare,
Our patchwork of living, so wildly rare.
With humor and wonder, let's stitch our delight,
For this crazy existence is a patchwork of light!

Ever-Unfolding Paths

In slippers worn, I seek my fate,
With coffee spills that seal my date.
Each twist and turn, I trip and slide,
Yet laughter's my trusty guide.

Thoughts like socks, they go astray,
One's in a drawer, the other's play.
I ponder life while eating pie,
And wonder just how time does fly.

There's wisdom in a funny dance,
Like tripping over love's first chance.
I stumble, chuckle, get back up,
And fill my days like a puppy's cup.

So here's to paths that zig and zag,
Life's parade of joy, a quirky brag.
With every slip, I learn to grin,
Embracing the chaos that draws us in.

Chronicles of Change

Each year I grow, but not quite wise,
My hair turns grey, I can't disguise.
With every wrinkle, I tell a tale,
Of trips to stores where socks turn pale.

I once was bold, now I just sigh,
Chasing things that make me cry.
A new diet starts but quickly fails,
While pizza sings its cheesy tales.

Life's like a book, with pages torn,
Each chapter starts with me forlorn.
Laughing at cards I forgot to send,
To friends I love, I'll never offend.

So here I sit, a work in jest,
With every hiccup, I'm quite impressed.
In change I find my daily chuckle,
Life's absurdity is my best cuddle.

Heartstrings of Humanity

We all have quirks, like hidden glares,
A need for snacks and comfy chairs.
I wear my heart where I can see,
On mismatched socks, just let it be.

Compassion's planted, like a seed,
That sprouts in jokes and laughter's need.
When life gets tough, we all just sway,
In silly games and childlike play.

With every awkward, loving hug,
We stitch our hearts, no need to shrug.
From coffee spills to tearful sighs,
We mend our souls with laughter's ties.

So let us bond in funky ways,
In life's great mess, let's sing and play.
Heartstrings tug in strange delight,
In this comedy, we take flight.

Whispered Insights

In quiet moments, wisdom peeks,
Through broken lamps and tangled beats.
I hear it whisper, 'Don't take it so,
Just dance like no one's watching, go!'

A squirrel once shared, 'Chase delight,
And climb your trees with all your might.'
With nutty thoughts and silly dreams,
Life's a swirl, or so it seems.

The lessons come in funny ways,
Like running late on laundry days.
I trip on thoughts that seem so grand,
But stubbing toes helps me to stand.

So lean in close for laughs and grins,
Embrace the quirks where joy begins.
With whispered insights in the breeze,
We find our paths beneath the trees.

The Unfinished Story

Once I wrote a tale one night,
But the plot got lost in the fridge's light.
Characters dance, then fall asleep,
In dreams they play, their secrets keep.

A twist here, a turn there, what a scene!
My pencil's broken, but I'm still keen.
Chapters skipped, and some out of tune,
Guess I'll finish it under the next full moon.

A hero jumps, then trips on a shoe,
Villains sip tea, as they plot what to do.
Notes are scattered like socks in a drawer,
This epic adventure? Oh, just ignore.

So here I am, half-done and spry,
With coffee spills as my loyal tie.
Come join the fun, it's all in jest,
An open book? More like a mess!

Harmony in Chaos

In a world where socks just run away,
And dishes sing 'wash me' day by day.
There's harmony found in every mess,
Like laughter mixed with a touch of stress.

A dance of dust bunnies, oh what a sight,
As I trip on laundry, 'tis my daily fight.
Rain falls like confetti upon my parade,
Life's a prank, and I'm its charade.

Between the hiccups and spilled drinks,
Are golden moments, or so it thinks.
Finding joy in the odd, the fright,
Like a cat that proudly claims the night.

So here's to chaos, my comrade true,
Mixing madness with a silly view.
In this circus, we twirl and sway,
With laughter leading the way to play.

The Art of Becoming

Each morning I wake, a blank canvas wide,
With coffee as my muse, I take my stride.
Brush in hand, I blend funny and wild,
Each stroke is a giggle, like a playful child.

An artist of antics, I scribble and roam,
Sketching the moments that feel like home.
Sometimes I splatter, sometimes I freeze,
But every creation is meant to please.

Transformation's the game, I'm a shape-shifting fool,
Today I'm a painter, tomorrow a pool.
With colors so bright, I'll color the skies,
In this work of progress, laughter is the prize.

So join my gallery of quirky delight,
Where the abstract meets the perfectly slight.
Each piece tells a tale of whimsy and grace,
In the art of becoming, we find our place.

Unveiled Realities

In the mirror, I see a face,
Making weird jokes, just in case.
Life's like a game of hide and seek,
I peek, I laugh, it's all quite bleak.

Bacon or tofu, which to choose?
Every meal is a chance to muse.
A dance with fate, a slip, a slide,
Wiping out with a goofy stride.

People come and people go,
No one knows why, though we put on a show.
With a wink and a nod, we walk the line,
Pretending we've got it all just fine.

So here's to the chaos, up and down,
This hilarious ride through fate's own town.
With every fumble and silly blunder,
We laugh aloud, it's pure wonder.

Symphony of Uncertainties

A note from life, a flat or sharp,
Playing in chords that never depart.
The rhythm breaks, it's all a mess,
Yet we're the stars in this silly dress.

Tangled thoughts like spaghetti strings,
In the sauce, we search for kings.
Who wrote the rules? Oh, what a laugh!
My to-do list? Just a quirky gaffe.

A sneeze at a wedding, a spill on the floor,
Life's funny moments, can't ask for more.
We juggle dreams with a wink and a grin,
While all onlookers just wonder where to begin.

So dance with the tunes of life's own plight,
Twirl through the chaos, hold on tight.
Find joy in the laughter and don't be shy,
When life takes a swing, just roll your eye.

Conversations with the Cosmos

Hey there, stars, what's your plan?
You twinkle like you know something I can't.
I ask the moon, but she just grins,
Says life's a show where no one wins.

Aliens, take me on a ride,
To worlds where all the lost dreams hide.
I'd trade a joke for a slice of pie,
Beam me up, Scotty, oh me, oh my!

Black holes and comets, making me feel,
In this universe, I might as well squeal.
What's at the end? A cosmic joke?
I question, chuckle, then laugh till I choke.

So here's to the chatter, the cosmic fun,
In a galactic bar, I'll buy everyone.
Raise your glass to the bizarre and wild,
For in this universe, we're all just a child.

Unfurling the Silk of Life

Life rolls out like a bright silk sheet,
But sometimes it's tangled at our feet.
With every fold, a wrinkle appears,
We laugh at the mess, suppressing our tears.

Threads of joy and strings of doubt,
Stitched together, what's it all about?
We fashion a dress for the grand parade,
With mismatched patterns that never fade.

The fabric pulls and sometimes tears,
Yet off we go with our quirky flares.
Life's just a tailor fitting us right,
Making sure our colors are always bright.

So let's dance on this luminous cloth,
Making each other laugh, a joyous etch.
For in all the tangle, we find our style,
Unfurling with laughter, a heartwarming smile.

Paradigms of Perspective

In a world full of pairs, we often lose our way,
Balancing on tightropes, smiling day by day.
Each wobble comes with lessons, wrapped in silly guise,
Life's a quirky circus, under clouds with sunny skies.

When you trip on your own feet, laugh instead of pout,
For every fall's a springboard, don't you dare doubt.
With pastels of confusion, we paint our canvas bright,
Masterpieces of mischief, obscured by charming light.

Mirages of Control

We chase the winds of fortune, like dogs chasing their tails,
Perspectives morph like jelly, within our grand sales.
We whisper sweet ambitions to the mirror of our fate,
Yet each reflection giggles, saying, "Ain't this great?"

A calendar of hopes hangs by a single thread,
Yet plan and sketch the future— and then laugh instead.
While order seems elusive, in chaos we delight,
As life serves up its punchlines, like a comedian's night.

Dances with Destiny

I tango with misfortune, slip on life's banana peel,
With every little twirl, I discover how to feel.
Destiny's a dance-off, where partners change each time,
And laughter's the reflection, in our clumsy little rhyme.

So spin me round in circles, like a dizzy little sprite,
With hiccups and with giggles, under neon moonlight.
Though fate may have its rhythm, it's our steps that make the show,
Each stumble is a story, in this life's grand ballet flow.

Silhouettes of the Self

In the shadows of the evening, our quirks begin to gleam,
Shapes of us evolving, like a dreamy, laughing dream.
We dress up in our foibles, wear them like a crown,
Exploring all the mishaps, with a smile, never frown.

Every flaw's a chapter, in the book of who we are,
Writing punchline punchlines, reaching for a star.
As we dance through our silhouettes, with humor as our guide,
We find joy in the journey, with laughter by our side.

Whispers of the Infinite Journey

In the morning light, I tripped on a shoe,
My coffee cup danced, oh what a view!
I pondered the meaning of socks left behind,
Is life just a riddle? I'm losing my mind.

A cat on the prowl took my sandwich away,
I chased after dreams that had gone out to play.
With laughter, I learned as I stumbled along,
That life's just a chorus, and I need a song.

I met a wise turtle who said with a grin,
"Take it slow, friend, let the chaos begin!"
With each silly moment, I gather my cheer,
The journey unfolds with each giggle and tear.

So here's to the chaos, the laughter, the fun,
For life's little secrets are better unsung.
With whimsy and wonder, we dance through the night,
In this grand, silly quest for what feels just right.

Lighthouses on Uncharted Seas

I sailed in a boat made from cardboard and dreams,
With a fish for a captain, or so it seems.
The waves told me stories of why I should float,
But my compass just spins, and it's stuck on a goat.

The sky cracked a joke, and the clouds burst in laughter,
I searched for the meaning in jokes, and disaster.
A whale called for tea while the seagulls played chess,
Navigating this life, I felt utter distress.

But then came a lighthouse, with lights shining bright,
It winked at the ocean, and said, "What a sight!"
"Just follow the giggles, they'll lead you to shore,
For life is a circus, don't ask for much more."

So I laughed at the waves, as they splashed with delight,
I let go of worries and danced through the night.
In this zany adventure, let all laughter soar,
Every shipwrecked moment, I cherish and adore.

Seasons of Self-Discovery

In spring, I found daisies that danced in a line,
They whispered sweet secrets and said, "You'll be fine."
With bees as my buddies, we crafted a plan,
To conquer the summer with sunscreen and tan.

But autumn arrived with a wardrobe of brown,
Leaves gathered like confetti, swirling around.
I pondered my choices, should I leap or stand still?
Laughter fell gently, like the leaves from the hill.

Then winter crept in with its challenging glint,
I slipped on the ice, what a humbling stint!
But snowmen just chuckled at my silly plight,
Revealing that life's just a snowball fight.

So here in the seasons, with each twist and turn,
I've learned that through laughter, there's much to discern.
With every misstep, I've come to decree,
Self-discovery's best when you dance with a bee.

Footprints in the Sand of Time

I walked on the beach with flip-flops askew,
Every step that I took, I felt like a fool.
The sand whispered secrets of those who have passed,
"Don't worry," it chuckled, "these moments won't last."

A crab scuttled by with a mischievous grin,
"Your plans for tomorrow? Just try them again!"
In this sandy confusion, I lost both my keys,
Yet the ocean just winked as it teased with the breeze.

Footprints like stories were washed out at sea,
But laughter remains in the soul, wild and free.
I built a tall castle that promptly fell down,
And wore a wet crown made of seaweed and frown.

So here's to the chaos of life on the shore,
With waves that keep crashing, it's never a bore.
Each footprint a giggle, each tumble a climb,
In this silly old riddle called footprints in time.

Embracing the Unfinished Canvas

Life's a sketch, a messy doodle,
Filled with laughs and quirky poodle.
Each day's a splash of paint so bright,
Who knew that blue could feel so right?

Mistakes are smudges, part of the game,
I tripped on joy, forgot my name.
Yet here I stand, with coffee in hand,
Creating art, not really planned.

Races of squirrels, a little run,
They teach us all how to have fun.
With crayons scattered all around,
Imperfections here, but joy is found.

Life's a canvas, still in play,
Every scribble leads the way.
No finish line, just vibrant cheer,
Keep adding colors, year by year.

The Dance of Imperfection

Slip on a banana, take a fall,
Life's a dance, we're not so tall.
Twirl to the left, bump to the right,
Laughter echoes through the night.

Steps may falter, toes may ache,
Yet we groove on, make no mistake.
A waltz of quirky, clumsy grace,
Each misstep, a warm embrace.

Tap shoes squeak, laughter rings,
Each goofy jig, our spirit sings.
Dance through doubts, let worries sway,
Imperfect steps make the best ballet.

So spin and laugh, don't take it hard,
Each awkward move, a cool discard.
With every twirl and silly cheer,
Embrace the chaos, hold it near.

Labyrinth of Choices

A fork in the road, what's it to be?
Ice cream or broccoli? Life's a spree!
Each path a riddle, a twisty maze,
Let's giggle and wander through this craze.

Do we wear stripes or polka dots?
The choices are many, some connect the dots.
Adventure awaits, a snack or a chat,
Why choose one when there's room for that?

Lost in the choices, we giggle a ton,
Should we walk or just run?—oh, what fun!
With every turn, a new chance awaits,
To laugh at the quirks that life demonstrates.

So leap into options, don't stay confined,
A whimsical journey of every kind.
For every meander brings forth delight,
In this labyrinth, let's take flight!

Colors of Unwritten Stories

In a world of crayons, what do we pick?
Pastels for dreams, or bold neon kick?
Drawing our tales, each hue screams loud,
Life's a canvas, let's paint it proud.

Scribbles of laughter, shades of surprise,
Every mistake: a masterpiece in disguise.
With every brush stroke, our tales unfold,
A riot of colors, stories untold.

Yellow for sunshine, grey for the gloom,
Blues when I trip and stumble in bloom.
Yet every tale shines in its own way,
With laughter and joy, we'll paint today.

So gather your colors, set your heart free,
Life's a mosaic—we're meant to be.
In every shade, let's find our cheer,
For unwritten stories are what we hold dear.

Portals to Awareness

I stepped through a door with a shoe on my head,
Thinking wisdom lived there, but it turned out to be lead.
The cat gave a chuckle, the dog rolled his eyes,
What was I seeking? Just fries and some pies!

I scribbled my dreams on a napkin, so neat,
But the waiter just laughed and brought me my meat.
Life's full of portals, each one with a joke,
Who knew that enlightenment came with a poke?

So I danced with my thoughts in a carnival flair,
Juggling confetti and doubts in the air.
Each laugh is a spark, a glimmer of chance,
To find in the chaos a whimsical dance.

I'll wear my confusion like a crown made of foam,
And march on this journey, wherever I roam.
With giggles and chuckles, I'll live with delight,
Finding treasures in jest, and the odd snack at night.

Eternal Questions

Why do socks disappear in the wash, I ask?
Are they off on adventures, a tricky old task?
Existential ponderings from the dryer of fate,
Maybe they're off to a sock party, how great!

Is there a plan or just chaos, I muse?
Like picking a flavor from jellybean hues?
Life's just a buffet with options galore,
And I'm here just sampling what's left at the store.

If I could ask answers, I'd query the cat,
Does she know all the secrets 'neath the soft mat?
But she just keeps napping, with a flick of her tail,
Maybe the key to it all is to relax and exhale.

Yet here I am, pondering each chewy bite,
Asking the moon if the sun sleeps at night.
With bites of confusion and laughter in tow,
Eternal the questions, yet how hard they don't flow!

Reflections in Still Water

I stared in the pond, saw a duck with a frown,
Was it my questions bringing him down?
He quacked for my thoughts—did I owe him a fee?
Or maybe he just wanted to chat over tea?

The clouds floated lazily, like thoughts in my head,
Could a cloud be a dream? Or just a soft bed?
With ripples of laughter, the water confides,
That answers are tricky, like fish that just hide.

Each splash was a giggle, a skimmer in light,
Reflections of what, beneath dark and bright.
The universe chuckles—it's all just a game,
And the water is winking; it's all part of the fame.

So I'll dance with the ducks, and we'll ponder together,
Life's just a riddle wrapped up in good weather.
As long as there's quacking and joy in the pool,
I'll embrace all the nonsense, and make that my rule!

Woven into the Struggle

Life's a tapestry woven with threads of odd fun,
Some colors are brilliant, and others just run.
I tug at the fibers, but they tangle and knot,
Finding wisdom in chaos, believe it or not!

I spin round in circles—what's knitting and purl?
Is there a pattern, or just a wild whirl?
The yarn sometimes whispers, "Just follow your nose,"
But why doesn't it guide me to chocolate or prose?

In a world full of looms, I'm just passing through,
With every mistake, I'm just twirling my view.
Threads snag on the moments, creating a mess,
But laughter's a color that brightens distress.

So here's to the weaving with colors so bold,
To fraying some edges and stories retold.
Through struggles and stitches, I'll dance with a grin,
For life's a big quilt, and I'm tucked right in!

Fragments of Existence

I woke up today, thought I'd be a star,
But then I tripped over my own guitar.
Life's like a puzzle, pieces askew,
Sometimes I question, is this really true?

My coffee's too cold, my toast is too burnt,
I laughed at my cat, who just looked concerned.
With dreams in my pocket and socks that don't match,
I dance in the kitchen, my life's quite a catch!

An email arrived, was it spam or delight?
I clicked on a link, now I'm lost in the night.
A meme made me chuckle, then I sighed with a grin,
If happiness is fleeting, why chase it like sin?

Each day is a canvas, splattered with cheer,
So I'll paint with my blunders, that's how I steer.
Laugh lines and mismatches, oh what a sight,
Give me joy in the chaos, I'll grasp it with might!

Threads of Unraveled Dreams

A dream told me secrets, with jelly on toast,
It whispered of futures, and I laughed the most.
I tried to unravel each thread with great care,
But they tangled my thoughts, left me quite bare.

I envisioned a castle, with ducks on the throne,
But it turned into chaos, and I sat there alone.
I found some lost socks, thrown out in the rain,
They said, "Join the circus!" It left me in pain.

A cat with a hat said, "Oh, what a ride!"
Life's like a rollercoaster, come enjoy the glide.
With dreams as my tickets, I smile through the rush,
And giggle at worries, in this great big hush.

So here's to the threads, all tangled and bright,
We dance through the mess, into the soft night.
Embrace all the dreams, whatever the scheme,
For life is a jigsaw, and joy is the theme!

In the Echo of Questions

I stumbled on answers, they laughed in my face,
They tickled my brain in a curious race.
Why is the sky blue? Why is toast so divine?
I ponder the riddles over sips of cheap wine.

The universe chuckles, it plays peek-a-boo,
With questions that spiral, like a twisty straw too.
"Am I just a shadow?" asks the old creaky chair,
"Or a million lost hours trapped in the air?"

Dropping some crumbs like breadcrumbs in time,
I follow my thoughts, they may turn out sublime.
Each uncertainty dances, a jig in my mind,
Maybe the answers are just left behind?

In the echo of laughter, I'll scribble my woes,
With puns and mishaps, life winks and it glows.
So if questions arise, just take them in stride,
Life's riddles and giggles, all part of the ride!

Pathways to Uncertainty

I took a wrong turn, my GPS froze,
Now I'm in a field, chasing some crows.
With pathways unclear, each step's like a dance,
Do I follow my gut or just leave it to chance?

The map's full of squiggles, like spaghetti on page,
I'm stuck in a maze, do I laugh or engage?
With twists and with turns, my compass spins wild,
But every wrong exit leaves me quite beguiled.

I met a wise frog, who croaked with delight,
"Life's like a jump, you just hope for good flight!"
With every leap forward, I trip on my shoes,
But who needs perfection? I'll relish the blues.

In pathways of chaos, I'll skip and I'll swerve,
Each misstep a story, each stumble a verve.
So here's to the journey, wherever it leads,
I'll chuckle through life, sowing playful seeds!

Echoes of the Unseen

In the mirror, I see my past,
A dance of socks, a laugh, a blast.
Chasing dreams with jellybeans,
Sorting snacks, or so it seems.

Time to eat, and then to play,
Fuzzy thoughts just drift away.
Wobbly truths, like jelly rolls,
Hold the secret, tickle souls.

Life's a game, with silly rules,
Where the wise often act like fools.
Count the stars or miss a train,
We find joy in the mundane.

Tickle fights with the cosmic jest,
Searching for what feels the best.
Laughter echoes through the night,
In the chaos, we take flight.

Heartbeats in a Silent World

In the hush of a quiet tone,
I've lost my keys, my thoughts have flown.
Counting beats and joyful sighs,
Wondering where the pizza lies.

With eyes wide open, I take a guess,
Life is truly a fashionable mess.
Fumbling along with mismatched shoes,
Who knew wisdom wore bright blues?

Silent hearts beat loud and proud,
In the stillness, I shout out loud.
Embrace the chaos, the laughter, the spins,
For that's where the joy truly begins.

With every heartbeat, new dances we make,
Life's a party, for goodness' sake!
So here's to the quirks, the mad and the mild,
In this wild ride, we are all still a child.

Notes from the Universe

A letter from stars said, "Oops, my bad!"
Gravity's always a little mad.
I dropped a comet, is that a sin?
What's that? Oh, don't let the fun begin!

A cosmic joke played in the night,
Chasing dreams that take flight.
Thought I had it, then I lost,
Finding joy in the silly cost.

Whispers of planets, a giggle or two,
While moons are spinning in a hula-hoop crew.
Earthlings dance on virtual screens,
Living lives like cartoon queens.

From black holes to pizza slices,
Life's a puzzle with plenty of vices.
So laugh loud, and let out a cheer,
In this grand universe, there's nothing to fear!

Stories Unfolding

Once upon a time in a busy street,
A cat wore glasses, oh, what a treat!
Bicycles danced in a wobbly parade,
While cupcakes plotted a sweet escapade.

A squirrel confessed it stole some mail,
With secret maps, it told a tale.
Each corner held a mystery bright,
In this chapter, nothing felt quite right.

Pages flip with a joyful twist,
In the library of dreams, we coexist.
Puppies ponder their place in the tale,
With wagging tails, they set sail.

From quirky friends to silly fates,
Life's a book of laughs and debates.
In every story, we find a piece,
Of heart, of humor, our souls' release.

Fractals of Existence

In a world of shapes and forms,
We dance on fractals, with all their charms.
Squares and circles, all in a twist,
Finding laughter in life's funny tryst.

From tiny ants to giant suns,
We ponder meaning while having fun.
In every zoom, a surprise awaits,
Life's jokes abound as it oscillates.

Curves that laugh and angles that smile,
We trace the paths, and stay awhile.
Each little piece a tale to tell,
In this grand puzzle, everything's swell.

So let's embrace this fractal spree,
With giggles dancing eternally.
In each dimension, joy is found,
With every heartbeat, laughter resounds.

Riddles of the Heart

Little riddles within our chest,
Playful puzzles, who'd guess the best?
Why do we giggle when love's on the line?
What makes the heart sing? Oh, simply divine!

Do we trip on our words like a clown at play?
Why does romance often lead us astray?
Behind every giggle lies a truth so bright,
What's hidden in shadows comes forth in delight.

Each beat is a riddle, a whimsical dance,
As we fumble and stumble, we're swept in a trance.
It's a circus of feelings, a carnival show,
In games of the heart, we all steal the glow.

So ponder with humor, let giggles arise,
With every new question, we'll open our eyes.
In a heart filled with riddles, joy is the key,
Unlocking the fun for you and for me!

Immersed in the Present

Here in the now, let's take a seat,
In this moment, life's quite a treat.
We juggle the minutes like clowns on a stage,
Laughing at time, turning every page.

With each passing second, let's giggle aloud,
Surrounded by present, we stand so proud.
Forget about worries, we'll just take a chance,
Life's a funny play; come join the dance!

What's past is a ghost, future's a dream,
This moment's a gift bursting at the seam.
So wear that grin, don your silliest hat,
In this joyful now, we discover, just that!

Let's toast to the present, a fine slice of fun,
With laughter as sunlight, we're each brightly spun.
So stay here beside me, in chuckles we dwell,
In the now, in the laughter, we both know it well.

Heart's Compass

With humor to guide, let's chart our course,
Navigating whims with love as our force.
This compass of laughter, oh, what a delight,
Leads us through the dark to the glow of the light.

In giggles and grins, our hearts lead the way,
Each twist and turn a wacky display.
Drawing arrows on maps made of joy,
Finding treasures in beings, not just a ploy.

When storms start to brew, let's dance in the rain,
With love as our anchor, there's nothing to gain.
Laughter is currency in this merry land,
With every heartbeat, let's take a stand.

So follow the compass, it's always on track,
With humor our guide, we'll never look back.
In the search for our treasure, we find it's quite clear,
The joy in the journey is all that we steer!

Echoes of the Everyday

Wake up, coffee spills, what a thrill,
We dance through chaos, oh what a drill.
The socks don't match, we laugh with glee,
Life's quirks are the best, just wait and see.

Plans fall apart, like a bad soufflé,
We navigate puzzles thrown our way.
A cat on a keyboard, typing with flair,
Reality's a joke, if you dare to care.

Bridges of Understanding

Conversations drift like balloons in the sky,
We bob and weave, laughing goodbye.
The awkward pauses, a comedic blog,
We bond over quips, like a well-placed fog.

Misunderstood texts lead to giggles galore,
We speculate meanings, then laugh some more.
Sharing a glance, in a crowded place,
Our stories entwine, a ridiculous race.

Tides of Intention

Plans shift like sand when the waves come near,
We sit on the shore, shedding a tear.
Life's bumpy ride has a comedic twist,
Embrace the absurd, it's too fun to miss.

Intentions like Jelly, they wobble and sway,
A jello mold of life, come what may.
Chasing our dreams, we trip over lines,
Falling with laughter, we'll be just fine.

Unwrapping Tomorrow

Tomorrow's a gift, in wrappings of cheer,
But oversleeping gifts us bags under here!
Unwrap the day with a grin so wide,
Life's silly moments, let's take in stride.

The calendar's a prankster, always in play,
With tricks up its sleeve, come what may.
We plan and we plot, but oh what a scene,
When surprises unfold, life's a meme!

Ebb and Flow of Purpose

Woke up today with a list in hand,
But first, I'll just lie here and plan.
Coffee's for champions, or so they say,
I'm still in pajamas, so maybe not today.

Passed a mirror, didn't quite recognize,
Who is this stranger with bedhead surprise?
I'll conquer the world—or at least my snack,
But first, let's find where I left my snack pack.

Life's a beach; I search for my flip-flops,
With soft waves of chores and laughter that pops.
I'll ride on this wave or maybe just float,
Forgetting my sadness, more joy than a coat.

In the ebb and flow, I find my delight,
With silly distractions that last through the night.
If purpose is fleeting, oh let it be so,
I'll chase it with giggles, wherever I go.

Labyrinth of Dreams

Riddles and puzzles in my sleep, oh boy,
Where's that cheese I hid? A holy grail toy!
Mapping my dreams like a curious chap,
But I keep getting lost in a giant cat nap.

A minotaur waits with a bowl of ice cream,
"Why chase your dreams? Just join me and scheme!"
I tumble through twists in this wacky parade,
Where my socks missing dance on a serenade.

Resume questing after a donut break,
Sliding on rainbows, for goodness' sake!
Forget all the seriousness, let's play pretend,
In this labyrinth of nonsense, it's fun without end.

Through the zigzags of stars, I cheerfully prance,
With jellybeans guiding my whimsical dance.
When dreams get too heavy, let laughter be light,
In this maze of my mind, I constantly write.

Kaleidoscope of Being

Colors of life swirl like candy in air,
One moment a giggle, the next a despair.
Twists and turns make my head spin around,
A carnival dream where silliness is found.

A patchwork of moments, of joy and of mess,
Sometimes I wear socks that don't quite express.
In shades of confusion, I'll dance through the haze,
With unicorns prancing in hilarious ways.

Flip the perspective; let's do a cartwheel,
In this jumbled-up image, oh what a big deal!
Laughing at troubles like jokes on a shelf,
In the kaleidoscope, I just might find myself.

So grab your kaleidoscope; twist it with glee,
For life's too absurd to be taken seriously.
A tapestry rich, so let's weave it wide,
In colors and laughter, we'll take life in stride.

Sunlight on a Winding Path

Stumbling along on this twisty lane,
With sunbeams that giggle, causing me pain.
Found a frog wearing goggles, what a delight,
He whispered, "No worries, you're doing alright!"

Each step feels wobbly as I skip and sway,
Where the flowers burst forth and dance in the fray.
A squirrel on a skateboard zooms past with pride,
While I trip on my shoelace again, oh my, wide!

The path may be winding, but laughter leads on,
Where bending the rules is always a con.
Sunlight's my guide, like a warm hug from above,
I follow the funny, the silly, the love.

With every turn, there's a giggle or two,
If life had a flavor, it'd taste like a stew.
So onward I wander, embracing the ride,
In sunlight and laughter, may I always abide.

Fragments of Infinity

I tripped on my dreams, quite a sight,
Peering through cosmos, it felt so right.
Coffee stains on the map of my brain,
Chasing stardust, but missing the train.

Life's puzzle, with pieces that twist,
I thought I was wise, but I just missed.
With every mistake, I learn to feel,
Laughing at plans that we dare to seal.

A dance in a circle, without a clue,
Hoping my partner won't step on my shoe.
Gravity's a joke I'm happy to tell,
As I tumble through thoughts, wishing them well.

The chaos of existence, oh what a blast,
Waving goodbye to the future and past.
In this quirky ride, I find my delight,
In fragments of infinity, I take flight.

Embracing the Imperfect

My socks never match, a fashion delight,
Yet I strut with a grin, feeling so bright.
Life's a cereal mix, some sweet, some bland,
Spilling happiness, isn't that grand?

I tried to bake cookies but burnt them to ash,
Yet laughter erupts in the midst of the crash.
With every flop, my spirit's unbent,
Perfectly flawed, what a great event!

Waltzing with chaos, I trip and I spin,
Finding the joy in the mess that I'm in.
With a wink to the world, I proudly declare,
Imperfect is perfect, and I do not care.

So here's to the stumbles, the slips, and the falls,
I'll take a bow, for right now, I'm enthralled.
Life's little blunders, like an awkward dance,
Are the quirkiest moments, so give them a chance.

Rivers of Change

Flowing through life like a river on fire,
Each current a laugh, an unending quire.
I tried to catch fish but caught a wet sock,
Yet here I am, still ticking the clock.

Oh, the twists and turns that I take every day,
With oars in my hands, I paddle my way.
Against all the tides, I'm still headed east,
Even if lunch is the only thing I feast.

As raindrops of chaos pit-pat my head,
I dance with the mud, leaving worries for dead.
Life is a splash, a wild little spree,
And I steer the boat, just my socks and me.

So let's toast to the rivers that never stand still,
With giggles and hiccups, we find our thrill.
Through wobbly waters, I joyfully roam,
In rivers of change, I've finally found home.

Finding Light in Shadows

I once met a shadow who promised me grace,
But it tripped on itself in a comical chase.
We giggled between the cracks of the sun,
In the odd little dance where shadows have fun.

In corners of doubt where confusion can dwell,
I found a small chuckle amidst all the swell.
Embraced by the quirks of a slightly dim light,
I learn to see joy in the depths of the night.

So here's to the shadows, those quirky old friends,
Who remind us that laughter is how joy begins.
When the world feels heavy, just lift up your feet,
And find the light hiding where darkness and laughter meet.

In puzzles and paradoxes, I choose to rejoice,
In a world full of chatter, I'll find my own voice.
So dance with your shadows and lighten your load,
For in their absurdity, the laughter flowed.

Beneath the Surface of Now

There's depth in my cup of Joe,
A universe swirls, don't you know?
Each sip is a journey I take,
With memories brewed, for humor's sake.

I ponder my socks, mismatched by fate,
A pair in the drawer, they can wait!
Sometimes life's answers are lost in the fray,
Like where I placed my keys yesterday.

Oh, ducks in the park play a game of tag,
While I look for meaning inside my bag.
Do they laugh at our worries, float by with ease?
If only my thoughts could float like the breeze!

Beneath the surface, I sometimes dive,
To find bits and pieces that help me survive.
So, I scribble my musings, on napkins and more,
Hoping to unlock that elusive door.

The Horizon Holds a Secret

The horizon glimmers, a curious tease,
Like a carrot dangled just out of reach.
Yet here I stand, quite content to reflect,
On the dance of the clouds and their silly effects.

I chase after sunsets while tripping on shoes,
Whistling old tunes that I never could choose.
Life's a stage, it seems, with no final act,
And I just play roles that make others react.

The seagulls squawk as if they know more,
About secrets of life from their perch on the shore.
"Just play," they would say, while stealing my fries,
And I laugh as I ponder their wise, fishy ties.

The horizon holds truths, though obscured they may be,
A balance of chaos, a grand mystery.
Life's never boring; it's a comic delight,
So I'll dance like a fool, then head home tonight.

Balancing Acts on Fragile Lines

I walk a fine line like a clown on a wire,
Each step a decision; I giggle, retire.
Life tosses me pies, sticky and bright,
Yet I juggle my worries with all of my might.

The world's a circus and I'm just a bear,
With dreams of a dance, and some magic in air.
But when I do flip, it's a laugh riot show,
'Cause who doesn't love when a jester says "Whoa!"

My balance is off, but I cheered the crowd,
With flips and with flops, I'm joyously loud.
The acts are absurd, but what can I say?
Life's best when it tumbles in humorous ways.

On fragile lines, I continue to tread,
With laughter and heart, life's a fun thread.
So, let's juggle our dreams and share in the jokes,
For each twist and turn, it's the fun that evokes.

Awakenings in Everyday Wonders

In waking moments, a kettle will sing,
Offering friendship in a hot, steamy ring.
Morning muffins with nuts, a delight,
I ponder their purpose, with every bite.

My cat leaps high, on shelves she will roam,
Surveying her kingdom, then calls it her home.
We act like we know, but we're really just groping,
For meaning in dish soap and stories we're hoping.

The neighbor's dog barks with endless resolve,
As if he holds truths we all need to solve.
With wagging tails and absurd little barks,
They teach me to play, igniting bright sparks.

In every odd corner, a nugget awaits,
Like socks gone astray, or catnip debates.
Awakenings surge in the mundane, it's true,
And laughter's the glue in this colorful brew.

Symphony of the Untold

In the orchestra of chance, we play,
With flutes made of dreams that won't decay.
The conductor sneezes, we all go flat,
Yet laughter erupts, imagine that!

Each violin whispers a secret theme,
While trombones slide down in a comedic dream.
We dance on the notes, a whimsical spree,
Conducting our fate with clumsy glee.

Embracing Uncertainty

Woke up today, what's for breakfast?
A guess; maybe cereal or bug-infested.
Flip a coin, and let fate decide,
My toast might fly! Oh, what a ride!

A job or a trip, a cat or a dog,
Life's a riddle, like a sunken log.
With each twist and turn, we trip and laugh,
The mix-up is gold, our heartfelt gaffe.

Kaleidoscope of Hopes

Hopes swirl around in a dizzying spin,
Like marbles in jars where they can't help but grin.
I wanted a house, but ended with a tent,
At least I've got snacks; my time's well spent!

Each dream is a color, bold and bright,
Some seem to fade out of sheer fright.
Yet the laughter we share in this vibrant mess,
Is more than enough, I must confess!

Reflections on a Wandering Heart

My heart is a traveler, passport in hand,
With stamps of mischief from every land.
Searching for wisdom in a sock drawer,
Wait, found a shoe! It's a metaphor!

Sailing on coffee, my compass is skewed,
Got lost in the fridge; thought I'd found food.
The journey's just laughter, no need for a map,
With friends on this ride, we nap and unwrap!